REMARKABLE RUGS

The Inspirational Art of Phoebe Hart

REMARKABLE RUGS

The Inspirational Art of Phoebe Hart

Harriet Hart

DOUBLE-BARRELLED
BOOKS

Published by Double-Barrelled Books

Double-Barrelled Books
www. double-barrelled-books.com

Editor
Caroline Clifton-Mogg

Design
Alfonso Iacurci and Hannah Dossary
Cultureshock Media

Copy Editor
Isabel Andrews

Production Manager
Nicola Vanstone
Cultureshock Media

Printed By
Butler, Tanner & Dennis

A CIP catalogue record for this book is available from the British Library
ISBN 978-0-9571500-4-1

In memory of Phoebe Hart

(1917–2007)

Introduction

Phoebe Hart's art is one of joyous exuberance. Her rugs and wall hangings are punctuated by explosions of colour and pattern, densely planted with trees and plants which hang heavy with fruit and flowers, as well as animals, birds and fish that dance – swooping and darting across the canvas. Expressive and imaginative, her work transforms the mundane canvas into a sun-filled painting worked in wool. Her inspiration is completely original and innovative, and drawn from two sharply contrasting worlds: the steel-bright, icy fire of the Ballets Russes or the sun-washed golden light of the Caribbean, particularly Jamaica – both touched with a lifelong love of American primitive art.

Born in 1917, the then Phoebe Foster was American by birth but brought up in England. After leaving school, and while debating whether to go to university or art school, she became – as were so many others at the time – enthralled by the productions of the wonderfully exotic Ballets Russes, the ballet company founded by Sergei Diaghilev in 1909 which caused a sensation wherever it played in the world. It is perhaps hard to conceive today just what an impact the Ballets Russes had on European audiences in the first half of the 20th century, and what an influence the fusion of avant-garde design, dance and music had on the relatively conventional theatre world of the time. This impact continued for many decades to come. The ballets had music composed by Stravinsky and Prokofiev, dance conceived and choreographed by the likes of Fokine, Massine and Nijinsky and sets and costumes designed by Léon Bakst and Natalia Goncharova, together with – later – by artists such as Derain, Picasso, Matisse and Miró; it is not surprising that the work of the Ballets Russes is still so potent today.

Although Diaghilev died in 1929, the Ballets Russes continued to perform under different guises, one of which was Colonel Wassily de Basil's Ballet Russe de Monte Carlo, founded in 1931. Among those who worked with de Basil on both revivals of the originals as well as new productions was the artist Vladimir Polunin, who had trained in Munich and Paris before leaving for England in 1911 in order to work with Diaghilev. Now, from his studio in Floral Street in Covent Garden, Polunin worked with de Basil on the design and set painting of the Ballet Russe de Monte Carlo productions in London.

Polunin was also the founder and head of the innovative Stage Decoration and Design course that was launched at the Slade School of Art in 1929. The course was legendary – the only one of its kind in the country – and in all of his students (who over the years included both Mary Fedden and Osbert Lancaster) he inspired a belief in colour and strong design. One of his pupils at the time wrote: "His department (known as the Zoo) provided a way to see things as a whole design while being a realm of fantasy".

Phoebe Foster signed up to this realm of fantasy, and soon found herself working in Polunin's studio on Ballet Russes sets. She later recalled that she and two other students painted backdrops: "New paintings were required for the revivals of old ballets, such as *Scheherazade* and Léon Bakst's *Petruchka*, as well as *Les Sylphides* for which a Corot landscape was adapted, *Boutique Fantasque* by André Derain, and *Le Tricorne* designed by Picasso. There were also new ballets – *Jeux d'Enfants*, for which Miró had done the designs, *Les Presages* designed by André Masson and *Le Beau Danube* for which a Constantin Guy sketch was adapted." It was a memorable time for balletomanes: "There was a magical quality to these performances in the six years preceding the Second World War – the famous Russian 'Baby Ballerinas,' Tamara Toumanova, Irina Baronova and Tatiana Riabouchinska, were enchanting English audiences as was the genius of Léonid Massine, dancer and choreographer."

The declaration of war in 1939 brought an abrupt halt to both balletic and artistic proceedings in the country, and Phoebe, who had married a naval officer who was tragically killed in action at sea soon after hostilities had begun, remained working in England for the duration. When peace was declared, she decided to leave England and move to America to live and work, and managed to find a passage on a cargo boat bound for New York. During the long Atlantic crossing she met a girl from Jamaica who invited her to the island for the summer. "This," Phoebe declared, "was an encounter that was to change my life."

So in June of that year, 1946, she flew from the United States to Jamaica to stay with her new friend.

Phoebe never forgot seeing Jamaica from the air during that first flight. She had had no idea what the island would be like; in her mind she expected somewhere sandy, treeless and flat surrounded by a turquoise sea; instead, as she flew over mountains and green forests, she watched the water below changing from aquamarine to sapphire. She was utterly enchanted: "What a change from my working life in Manhattan – with its cold winters, crowded subways, and nowhere to really call home – to the warmth and colour of Jamaica, its friendly people, and mountains, tropical flowers, seashore and soft rain."

She drove through the hills where roadside vendors were selling big bundles of beautiful ground orchids and exotic fruit artistically arranged on sticks. There were oranges, ortaniques, tangerines, globular pale green and dark purple star apples, which when cut in half revealed a star pattern of seeds; brown naseberries, tasting of brown sugar and gineps, that were like large pale green grapes with a tough skin and a delicious jelly-like flesh.

Phoebe was entranced as never before: "Those green hills and the marvellous, irregular, mountainous landscape, the patches of rain forest, pasture land and big clumps of tall bamboos like green ostrich feathers; deep valleys, ridges with a few tiny houses clinging to their

edges, threaded through by little dirt roads. And the red soil and cattle land of St Ann and the cane fields. Oh how I loved this wonderful, wonderful country!"

There, in Jamaica, she met Herbert Hart, who was to be her second husband. They married that autumn, and she moved to Jamaica, where she lived for nearly forty years.

The effect of this new life on her artistic imagination was immense, for who could not be inspired in the soft, warm, sun-filled light of the Caribbean, by the paint-box blue of the sea, the iridescent flash of a humming bird's wings or the extravagant spread of a hibiscus flower? It was here that she first started to create designs for needlework, specifically working with the embroidery workshop Carawak Crafts, one of several rehabilitation schemes for post-tubercular patients who were there to be taught to embroider on table linen, guest towels and aprons. "The embroidery patterns', Phoebe said, "were so dull and outmoded that I was asked if I could design some new patterns for them." She felt that they should use what could be seen all around them – some of the fascinating and varied birdlife (there are over three hundred species in Jamaica, several of which are found only on the island) as well as the tropical fish and marine landscape of the coral reef, the flowers, fruits and insects, all of which were incorporated in bright, tropical colours into the Carawak Crafts designs.

"Most of our workers had no embroidery skills and had to be taught," Phoebe recalled. "I too had none and found that I had to learn to embroider, however inexpertly, in order for them to translate the designs into stitches; coloured sketches just didn't work. My first efforts were clumsy, but good enough to get across how to place and blend colours and stitches. Our products became popular, we increased our output; we exported to the Bahamas and Canada and I designed some embroidered linen dresses that were sold at Liberty's in London. And it was our work that was chosen by the Jamaican Government to present to the Queen on her two visits to Jamaica – for the first visit, a set of pale blue table mats with an embroidered edge of twigs and leaves and one of Jamaica's indigenous birds on each mat. For her second visit, dark green silk embroidered with orchids."

Opposite: Detail from *Birds of Jamaica* (p.30)

the
ISLAND
of
JAMAICA
&
the 24 BIRDS
ONLY found there

Over the next twenty years, although still based in Jamaica, Phoebe visited England periodically and often stayed with Irene Andrews, a friend, who was designing and making rugs: "beautiful rugs to her own design, inspired by antique Spanish and Portuguese carpets. Irene used a Bargello stitch – brick-stitch – which not only covers the canvas more readily than tent stitch, but does not pull it out of shape, being a straight stitch rather than diagonal. She sourced her wool from a nearby carpet factory – one hundred per cent wool and a wide range of varied colours, and supplemented these with Appleton crewel wool. She worked out her designs on eight squares to the inch graph paper – the same scale as her canvas."

Phoebe was hooked: "so back home in Jamaica, I attempted my first piece of work – an ambitious project – a stair carpet for our house there – worked in tent stitch and in black and white and two shades of grey."

As a child, Phoebe had been much influenced by an aunt in America who collected early American naive art – in particular, hooked rag rugs and painted furniture. She was fascinated by the way that early pioneers used everything around them to create objects of practicality and often great beauty, from the woven patterned bedspreads and quilts made from scraps of old shirts and dresses to the pieces of painted furniture and floor cloths. "Since I was so attracted to the early American rugs with their folk art designs, my next project after the stair carpet was a large rug for our bedroom, based on the Caswell Carpet, a famous primitive embroidered American rug, made in the early 19th century, and now in the Metropolitan Museum, New York. Dark brown was the colour scheme for the bedroom, so when I came across a picture of the Caswell Carpet with its eighty different squares, all with varying shades of dark brown background and delightful naive but harmonious designs, I adapted eighteen of the individual designs and from these, made a rug."

"A visitor to the house saw the rug and wanted to buy it. He turned out to be a dealer in early Americana. I made another for him – which he kept – but he then inspired me to begin making rugs to sell. Through him and through a folk art gallery in London I produced many more rugs, all of them my own design, but always in the early American folk art style."

Phoebe stitched and sold several other rugs through dealers and shops but soon discovered that it was more fun – as well as more profitable – to undertake private commissions. So she began to design and make rugs that featured particular houses, animals, flora and fauna as well as rugs for anniversaries and birthdays. The commissions may have seemed straightforward but now, through her work, Phoebe Hart was beginning to move away from what she herself called "the somewhat naive folk art style" towards a new imaginative vision based on her own artistic inspiration.

During the following years, Phoebe Hart's unique and innovative style developed yet further and was always fused with an element of whimsical poetic fancy. Her designs displayed a creative tension, a cultural fusion of east and west, north and south. More significantly, there was also a juxtaposition of decorative and artistic influences: on the one hand a lifelong interest in the purity of American naïve art, on the other the explosive but disciplined passion of the Ballets Russes. All were coloured by the deep richness and slow-stepping beauty of Caribbean natural life. Through such unions is originality born.

Phoebe Hart working on one of her rugs in London, in 1997.
© Peter Trievnor

Techniques

Phoebe Hart (who often rose at dawn to work on her rugs) usually used canvas with five or eight holes to the inch. As far as the design went, she said herself that she was not of the temperament to work out her designs on graph paper with endless counting of stitches. Instead, she preferred to draw the design onto a white sheet of paper – usually tracing or baking paper – using charcoal, which could be easily rubbed out. Once satisfied with the design, she would lay the canvas on top and go over it with a permanent black felt pen. Sometimes, when the light was bad, she would place the drawing onto a sheet of glass that was lit from below, thus making it easier to see through the canvas.

If absolutely necessary (because there was no way that she could visit the subject), Phoebe would design and make the rug from photographs – the colonial farmhouse on page 126 is one such example; here, she drew the building onto the canvas using photographs as her guide.

Phoebe never painted the canvas directly, but sometimes would make a coloured sketch on a separate piece of paper to work out the colours, often working on it as she went along, a technique which always made the work more interesting. She would often put in all the details of the rug before finally deciding on the background colour.

Phoebe felt that her sewing technique was unique, writing in 1997: "I have not seen, nor come across in any needlework book, a similar method of sewing to my own – combining crewel embroidery with needlepoint – but no doubt others have done it. I use crewel embroidery stitches like 'long-and-short' stitches and stem stitch for the detailed areas of design such as flowers, foliage, etc, giving a fluid look that is less controlled by the grid of the canvas. For the background, I use the Bargello stitch – brick-stitch – a vertical or straight stitch which is more versatile than a diagonal one; straight stitching also means that the canvas does not become distorted or skewed sideways as can happen when a continental or half-cross stitch is used. A tent stitch is used

for outlining, and a plaited stitch for edging the rug, inside of which there are usually two or more rows of a slanting herringbone stitch. These five comprise my repertory." Once finished, the rugs had to be 'blocked' by damping and nailing to a board to dry so that they became straight and flat.

Most of the wool that Phoebe Hart used was carpet wool from factories such as the Wilton Royal Carpet factory in Wiltshire. Appleton crewel wool was also used, and this can be obtained today from many needlework shops such as the Royal School of Needlework (www. royal-needlework.org.uk) and Lenham Needlecraft (www. lenhamneedlecraft.com).

She was, rightly, proud of the work that went into making the rugs, both large and small: "The average size of my rugs is around 4x5 feet and the wall hangings are usually around 3'6" by 2'6", but I have done larger rugs – I think the largest is one in Jamaica of a mermaid and a merman, shells and fish – it is about 9x7 feet. I have also done small things like cushions and church kneelers, each individual in design. Except for a brief period when I had a little help with edges and background, every stitch has been taken by me. I have had work hanging in the UK, the USA, Italy, Denmark, Jamaica, Trinidad, Tobago and for a few years, until the owner moved to Washington DC, in Soviet Russia!"

Right: Spring Greens (p.102); Summer Red and Pink (p.96)

Opposite: Detail from Rockledge Farm (p.126)

The Borders

The borders and surrounds of Phoebe Hart's rugs are an important, indeed integral, part of each design. Not only do they act as a frame to the central design, they also inform and embellish the ideas behind the design, sometimes by complementing the central theme, at other times by contrasting the outer with the inner. The designs were often created in the moment, and inspiration came from many different quarters. Her range of sources was wide and included academic works – she had an extensive library of design reference books and studied dictionaries of design such as The Grammar of Ornament, published in 1856 by the architect and designer Owen Jones, which remains the definitive encyclopaedia of flat pattern with carefully drawn examples from every culture in the East and West. Further inspiration came from early examples of craft work, such as the border that is patently inspired by the delicacy of a piece of Victorian bead work (p.50).

Italian art was a pervading influence. One border shown here is clearly influenced by *pietre dure*, the Italian technique of using semi-precious stones in an elaborate mosaic (p.78); another echoes the work of the great Renaissance ceramicist della Robbia – an artist much admired by Phoebe Hart.

There are various common themes that echo through different designs – the trellis, the endless knot and the swastika. And Phoebe was also, like every true artist, inspired by what she saw around her. A vegetable rug has a border of – what else – vegetables, including fat bulbs of garlic, round, sunny tomatoes, spring onions, peas, radishes and cauliflower. Another border, this time framing a rug that shows the native birds of Jamaica, is an airy design of bamboo trees, the leaves and stems delicate around the bright hues of the birds.

Not content with one motif on a border, Phoebe Hart often used two or more for her rugs and wall hangings. A plaited stitch would hold the folded edge of the canvas in place, which was then ameliorated by one or two rows of single colour stripes, rather like the colour wash lines on the paper mount around a picture. Within this basic border might then have been added particular motifs that related more closely to the subject of the rug – perhaps vine leaves snaking upwards or garlands of flowers artfully arranged – always depicted in fine and sharp detail.

For the depth of detail is as important a part of Phoebe Hart's rugs as the overall theme. Each bird, butterfly and fish was studied and copied in every last accurate detail – not always to scale of course, that depended on the exigencies of the design – but always correct in the colouring of the plumage or the markings of the shell, each element carefully and remarkably translated onto the canvas. Animals in particular were recorded with gimlet-eyed accuracy, their personalities and foibles miraculously portrayed in wool rather than paint.

Right: Partridges (p.50) depicted in the Scottish countryside

Opposite: The Zodiac Rug (p.156), in which the details of the astrological and the four elements are imaginitive and inspired

Opposite: The border on Ribbons and Grapes (p.78) is complex and fluid in design

Top right: A linear border on white Cockatoos (p.52)

Bottom right: A suitably bucolic border from Spring Cottage (p.116)

Within a basic border, Phoebe added motifs that related to the subject of the rug – snaking vine leaves or garlands of flowers.

Islands of the sun

From the splashes of brightness on the darting fish of the reef, to the dark, dense greens of the forest and the blue, blue, blue of the sea – this is the colour-filled Caribbean, and Phoebe Hart was enthralled and endlessly inspired by everything to be seen there.

Tobago House, 1996
Set on a beautiful island close to the sea, where coral reefs shelter fish – squirrel, parrot, sergeant majors, and rock beauties.

Shells, 1993
One of a pair of shell rugs, each shell correct in shape, colour and fine detail, although the scale is determined by the overall design.

Birds of Jamaica, 1997
As a keen birdwatcher, Phoebe Hart was entranced by the twenty four endemic species of birds found in Jamaica, and depicted them here
with a map of the island, and surrounded by a border of bamboo. (107 × 173cm)

The Caribbean, 1984
Flying fish skim through the air, whilst below, around the reef, rock beauties, and squirrel fish graze. (145 × 114cm)

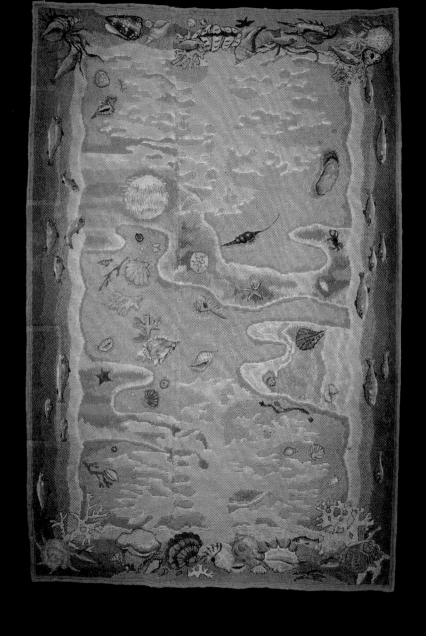

Sea, sand, shells and moon, 1983

Inspired by the shell-scattered seashore along the North coast of Jamaica, the full moon is reflected in the pool of water left by the retreating waves. (229 × 153cm)

Shells, 1993
The companion to the rug on page 26, Phoebe Hart employed the traditional Arbrash technique for both rugs to effect subtle changes in the colours of the basic ground.

On the wing

For bird lovers, of whom Phoebe Hart was certainly one, the birds of the Caribbean are more than merely birds – their iridescent colours, their unique beauty – that of their plumage, their flight, their very being – all these things are constantly captivating and entrancing.

Shawn's Birds, 1980
Based on a painting by the daughter of a friend, a flock of goldfinches sit in serried ranks in a wide-branched tree.
Unusually, the background colours have been achieved by stitching with strips of fabric rather than with wool. (137 × 100cm)

Flowers, fruit and birds, 1988
Designed to be viewed from both sides, this is a fruit and flower melange, combining the tropical and the temperate, with pineapple
and watermelon beside roses and clematis. The colour palette reflects the strong colours admired in the 19th century. (127 × 160cm)

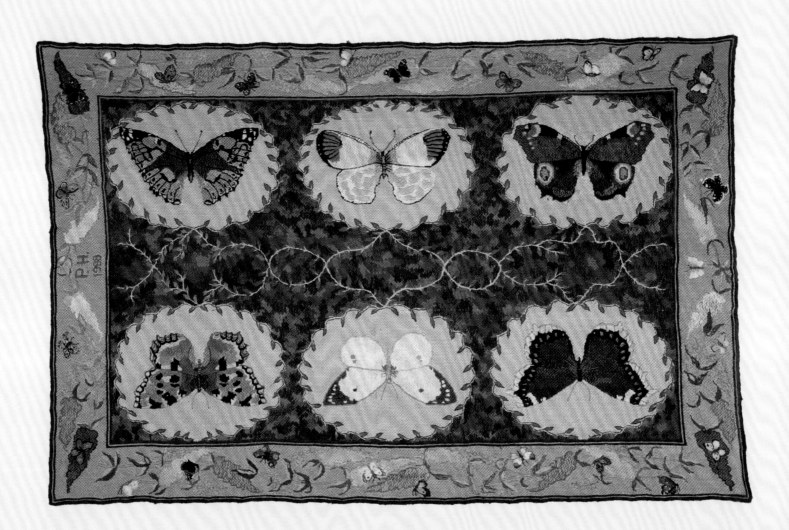

Butterflies and Buddleia, 1988
Depicted in fine detail, the butterflies here include the Camberwell Beauty, Clouded Yellow, Painted Lady and the Peacock.
The background is a subtle, mottled brown-amber, and the border is dominated by the buddleia – the butterfly bush.

Partridges, 1978
Partridges nest amongst daisies in the open farming country side of Fife, Scotland. The intricate border,
set with roses is inspired by Victorian bead work. (69 × 104cm)

White Cockatoos, 1990
Possibly inspired by a trip to Australia, is this bold design of white cockatoos perched in a banana tree.

A *Peaceable Bestiary*

Benign lions and haughty cats, saucer-eyed spaniels and dignified horses – Phoebe Hart had an empathy with all animals and was always able to brilliantly convey on canvas their unique personalities, characters and quirks.

Horses under a chestnut tree, 1978
A design inspired by early American naive art, in which Phoebe Hart was interested from an early age.
The deliberate lack of perspective and proportion is charming.

Jenny, 1980
A true-to-life portrait of a much-loved cat sitting in her garden. The border has been designed as a traditional picture frame, befitting the formal portrait within.

Lion and Lioness, 1978

The design is based on an Early American folk art painting; in a further gesture to the primitive tradition, the ground on which the lions are standing is made from torn up strips of fabric, as employed by many early rag rug makers. (64 × 127 cm)

Cat in a Breadfruit Tree, 1982
The detailed lines of the breadfruit tree leaves are painterly in their execution, and the cat is one who walks alone,
rather than someone's favourite pet. The background is of a Jamaican rural landscape, and the border, with its different shades
of green is almost three-dimensional. (92 × 61cm)

Katy, 1981
Katy was a dog whose home was in the parish of Westmoreland in Jamaica, on Chiltern, a cattle property,
surrounded by pastures and hillside. The border is of a jade vine weaving through trellis.

Bears and Dolphins, 1985
In the manner of a coat-of-arms, the rug depicts bears signifying strength, grapes abundance and dolphins, charity and love. (137 × 122cm)

J&D

Klee, 1982
A handsome black and white cat named Klee has been suitably honoured with a background of fish, birds
and a full moon, that pays homage to the painter Paul Klee. (81 × 130cm)

The Lion, 1977

An early rug in Phoebe Hart's career, made for her son Jeremy. Influenced by early American folk art, it depicts a handsome lion,
a soldier and domed buildings in the background, bordered with primitive leaves and flowers.

Flowery Work

Artists have always found in inspiration in flowers and Phoebe Hart was no exception. From English garden flowers to tropical vines and exotic blooms, every type of bloom and blossom were, in her rugs, incorporated into garlands and bunches, bouquets and sprays.

Ribbons and Grapes, 1995
A combination of decorative styles, with a central motif inspired by an Italian Pietra Dura table top, whilst the border is also
reminiscent of a stone inlay but used in a more fluid manner. The subtle background mimics the Arbrash colour variations found
in some antique carpets. (137 × 203cm)

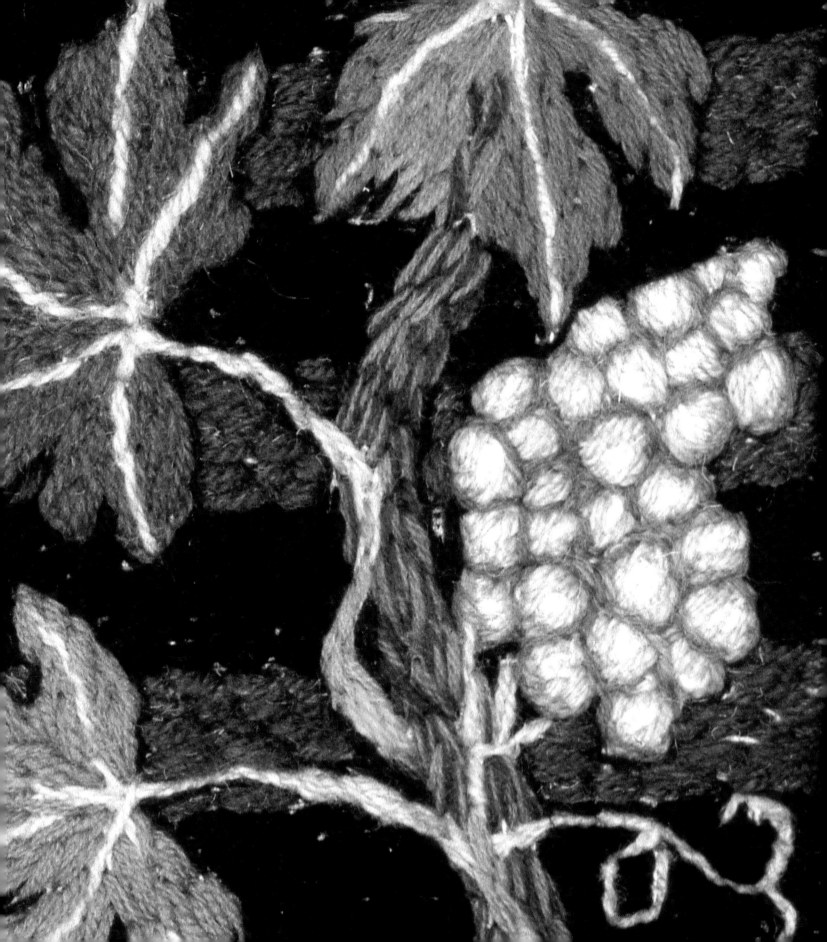

Bricks and Bulbs, 1997
A favourite piece of Phoebe Hart's, this large wall hanging depicts spring bulbs such as hyacinth, narcissi, muscari and tulips.
Each square is divided by a brick border, giving the effect of a two-dimensional parterre or paved bed. (137 × 183 cm)

The Caswell Carpet, 1975
Inspired by a large, embroidered square carpet of the same name, made between 1832 and 1835 and now in the Metropolitan Museum of New York. Made for the family home in Jamaica, Phoebe Hart chose eighteen squares from the original and adapted them to fit.

The Fruitful Harvest

From sweet, chubby tomatoes to aristocratic asparagus, and ripe, red strawberries and cherries, Phoebe Hart depicted fruit and vegetables in a succulent and delicate way, elevating humble vegetables and fruit into works of art.

Vegetables on Blue, 1993
Asked to design a rug of vegetables on a blue background, Phoebe Hart decided to use as many blues as she could, and twenty five varieties of vegetables. A della Robbia inspired border frames the charming composition. (213 × 168 cm)

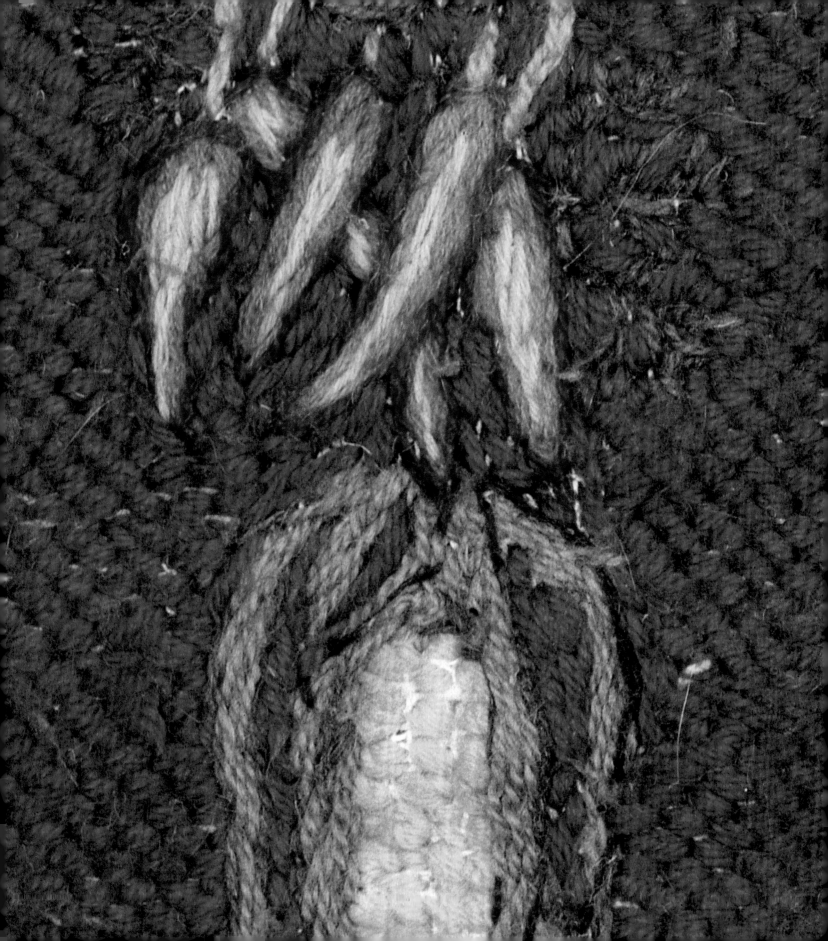

Summer Red and Pink
Red toned fruit and vegetables with rhubarb as the centre piece. Strawberries, cherries, red apples and a watermelon jostle
with radicchio, aubergine, tomatoes and beetroot. Red pears mix with a basket of roses. (92 × 74cm)

The Fruitful Harvest

Winter Whites
An all-white composition including leeks, cauliflower, garlic, parsnips, turnips white cherries, mushrooms and grapes. (92 × 74 cm)

The Fruitful Harvest

Spring Greens
The fresh greens of spring make up this design with cucumber, cabbage, kohlrabi, broccoli, marrow, and a Brussels sprout plant which towers above. Peas, okra and asparagus complete the design. (92 × 74cm)

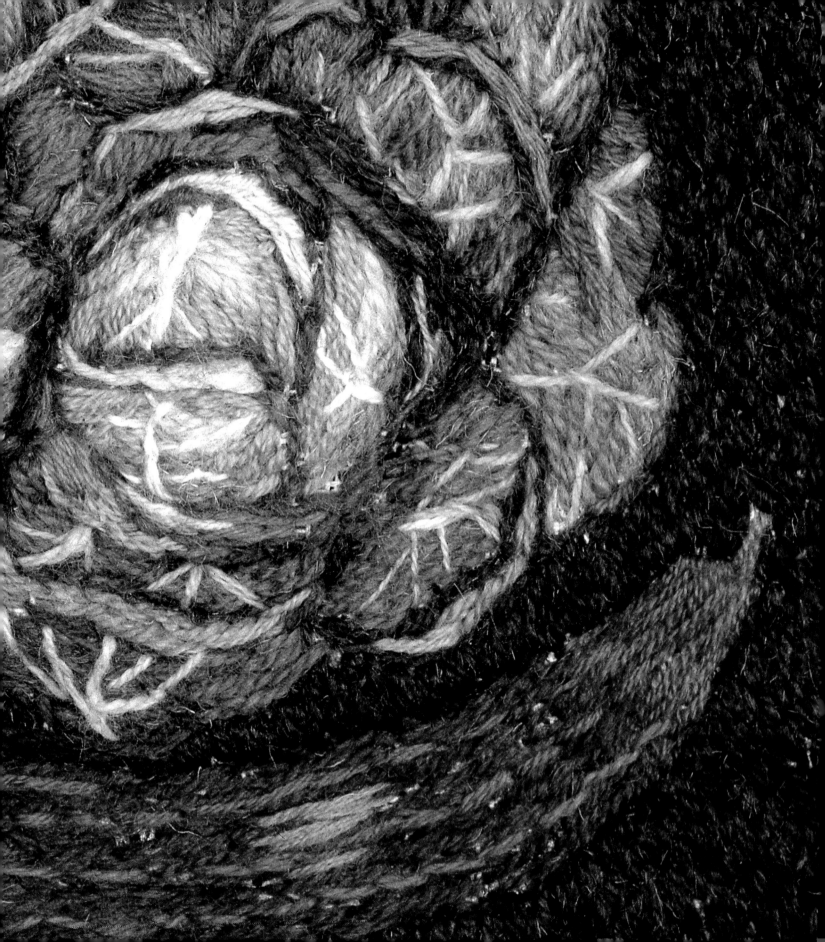

Vegetables on Black, 1995
After designing the seasonal hangings, Phoebe Hart wanted to experiment further with the varied colour and shapes of vegetables.
Here, the dramatic black background sets off marrow, pumpkin and gourds as well as cauliflower, mushrooms, lettuce and asparagus.

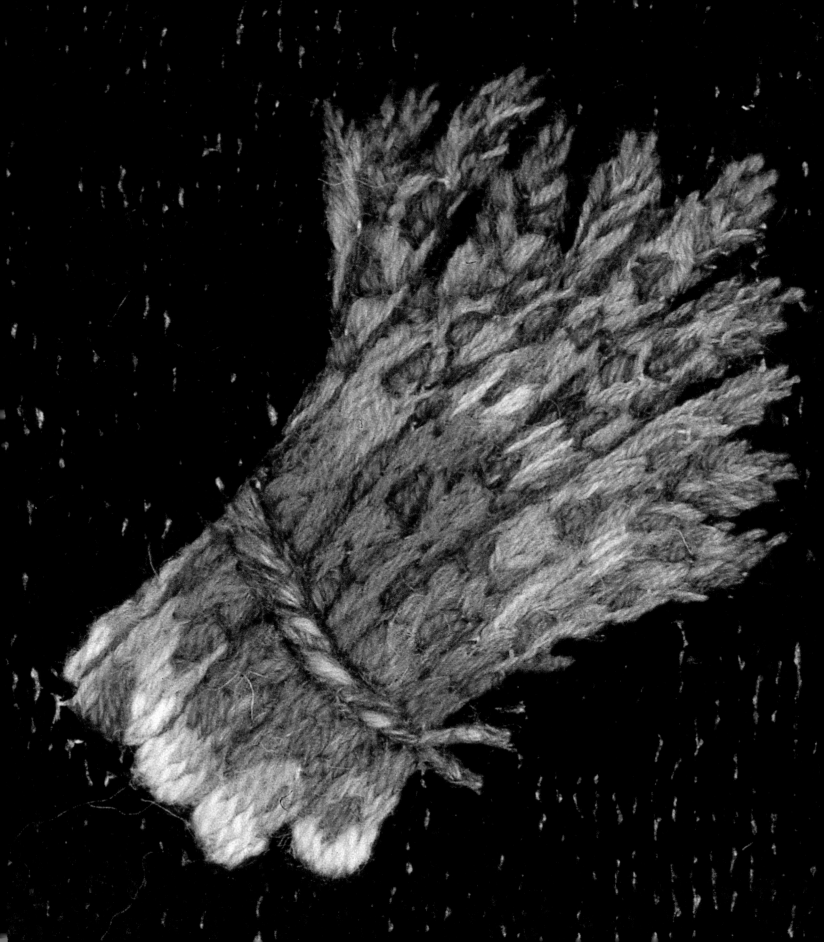

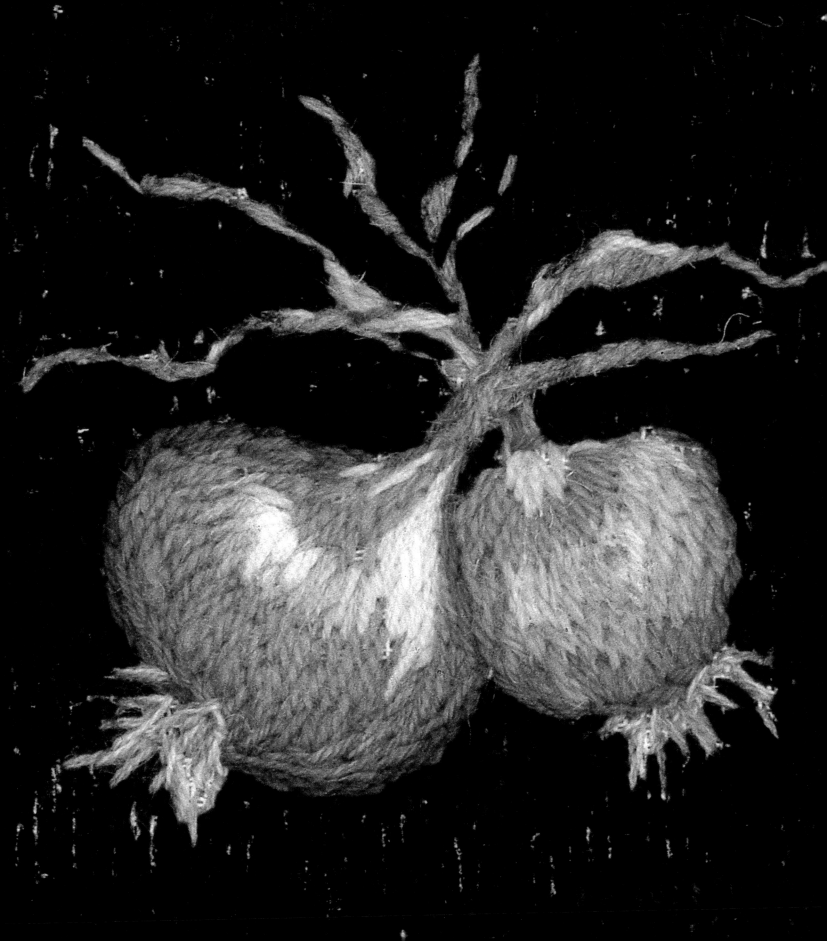

Green Man

For hundreds of years, a symbol of rebirth and the coming of Spring, the Green Man is always depicted with leaves, branches or vines.
Here, he emerges from oak, beech and ivy leaves; the surrounding Gothic arch of branches and blossom suggests a church. (94 × 152cm)

The Fruitful Harvest

Flower of the Month Calendar, 1980
This rug was commissioned by the owner of a Sussex cottage, and a cat called Juniper. The squares that surround Juniper show each month
and its associated fruits and flowers – strawberries in June, a birds nest in May and a sunflower in September (103 × 168cm)

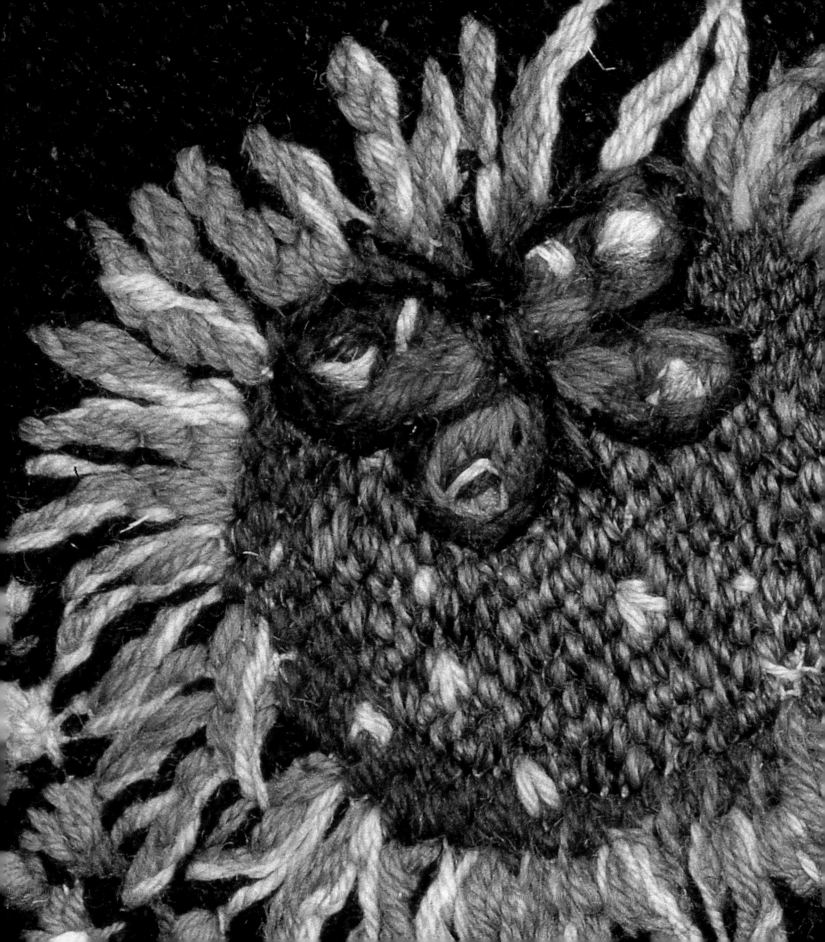

The House Beautiful

The idea of home is important,
and through her rugs Phoebe Hart
immortalised many different ideas
of home, from low plantation
houses, to country cottages;
from picturesque farms to solid
mansions, every one a picture.

Spring Cottage, 1987

A cottage with a garden of topiary and gambolling lambs. From the central 'Tree of Life' spring flowers grow
from the trunk – fritillaries, snowdrops, muscari, and tulips. (102 × 76cm)

Jamaican House, 1980
The old wooden houses in Jamaica are brightly painted with cedar shingle roofs, verandahs and gingerbread fretwork and surrounded with frangipani and hibiscus. Here, local birds hover: the streamer-tailed hummingbird, banana quit and the saffron finch. (94 × 127cm)

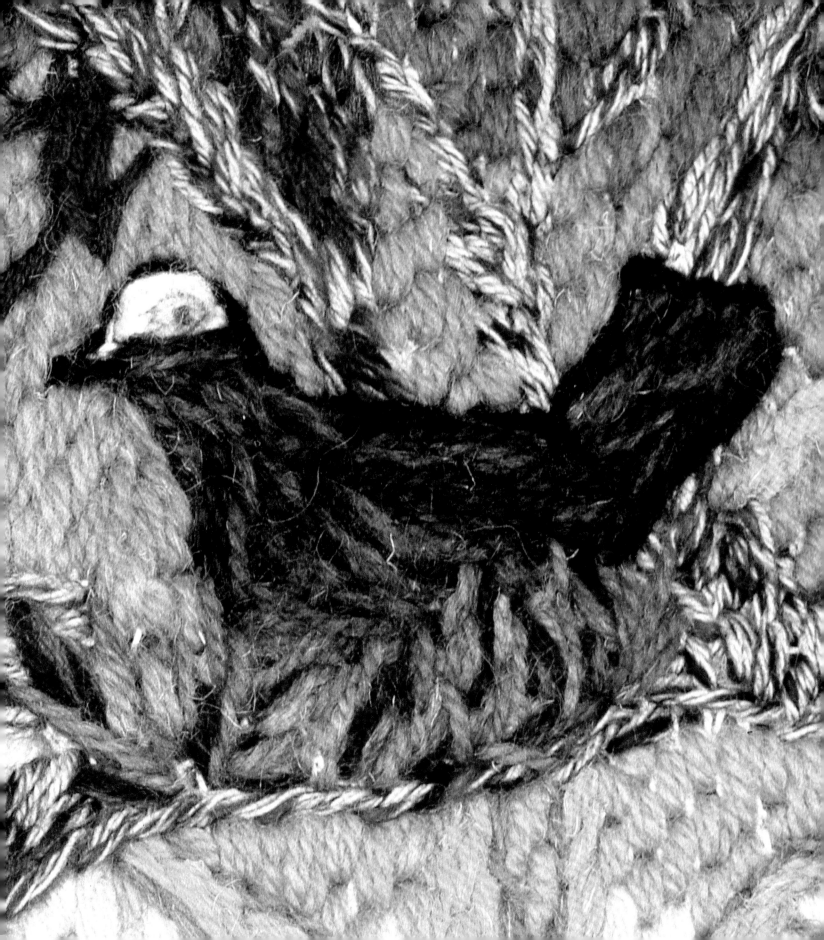

Banana Walk, 1979
Made to celebrate daughter Harriet's 21st birthday, the depiction is of Harriet's childhood home, with a lake and a garden filled with datura, frangipani and passion flowers, surrounded by some of the animals in residence during the 15 years the Hart family lived there.

HARRIET
on being
21

Rockledge Farm, 1981
Rockledge Farm in Vermont dates from 1799, and is shown here with farm animals as well as wild animals
such as a chipmunk with a basket of strawberries.

The Chapel, 1985

An old chapel converted into a house, complete with Gothic arches and a formal bed of tulips and fruit trees.
The surrounding panels detail a stone window, drinking trough, some ruins and a font.

Ardlui, 1970

Ardlui is an old, traditional Jamaican wooden house with gables and porch trimmed with fretwork, which once stood in Kingston.
Here, set into a decorative roundel, it is surrounded with a scene inspired by the famous early American 'Peaceable Kingdom' paintings.

A French House, 1984
With its stone walls, blue shutters and dovecote in the roof, this is French perfection, where the dogs
on their stone plinth echo the tones of the clouds. (122 × 155 cm)

In Celebration

Perhaps the finest type of inspiration comes from a celebration – a birthday, a marriage, a golden wedding, a life. Phoebe Hart found inspiration in the minutiae of others' lives and in personal moments and places of importance.

In Celebration

Washington DC, 1998

An all-American rug celebrates Independence Day with fireworks and apple pie.Chesapeake Bay sits centre stage,
surrounded by all-American birds such as the red cardinal, blue jay, mocking bird and American robin.

A 40th Anniversary
Moments and significant places and things are documented here, from the lighthouse where the couple met
to a favourite car and Philadelphia's Liberty Bell.

An 18th Birthday, 1991
Memorable moments and things: a much-played cello and favourite cats, coupled with a summary
of a life so far through a childhood and beyond. (107 × 76 cm)

A Golden wedding, 1996
Full of incident and memories, this golden wedding wall hanging combines momentous places including
references to an astrophysicist son and writer daughter.

Eliza and Neil's Wedding, 2001
A marriage between England and Scotland, with symbolic hand fasting, rainbow, angels, bells and roses, and of course hearts.

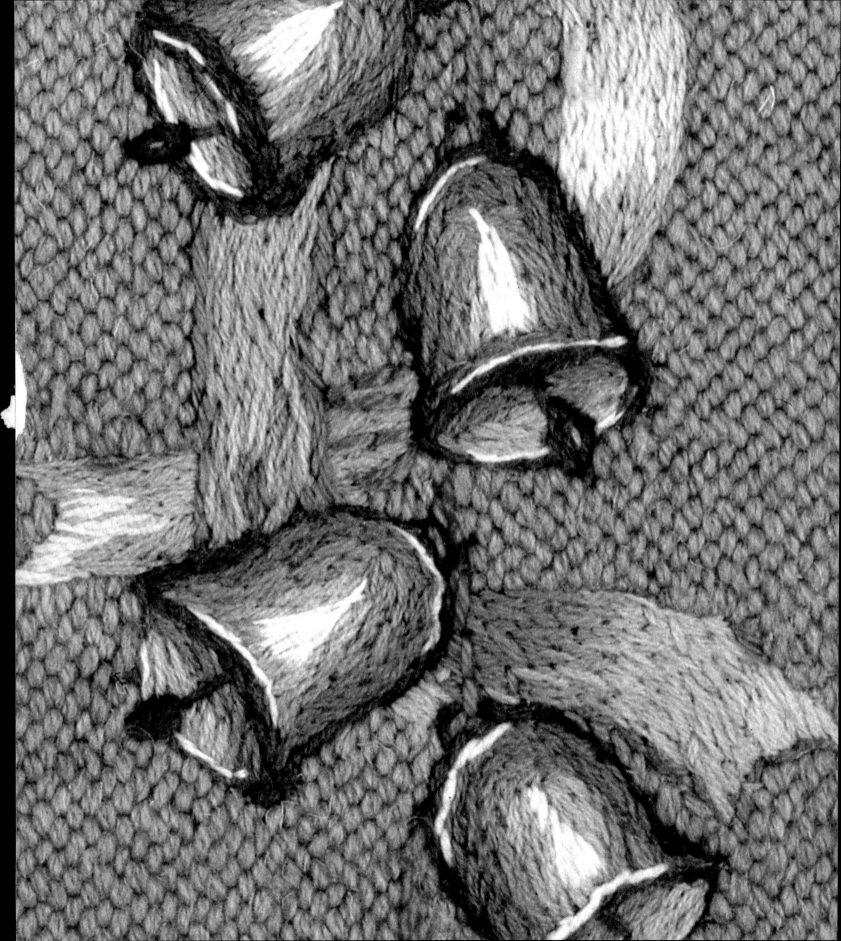

The Zodiac, 1989
Following paintings that Phoebe Hart had done of individual Zodiac signs, she designed and made a magnificent Zodiac rug, with all twelve
signs and their constellations set in a starry background surrounded by the four elements. (152 × 152cm)

Acknowledgements

The idea for this book came from Caroline Clifton-Mogg, Phoebe's god-daughter, and co-founder of Double-Barrelled Books. Caroline has been the driving force behind the whole project. It is her vision, determination, and hard work that has brought *Remarkable Rugs* into being.

I also wish to thank Phoebe's great friend Annie McCaffry, for her helpful suggestions, corrections, and general tub-thumping enthusiasm, and my brother Jeremy Hart, for his encouragement and support.

Great thanks must also go to the many collectors around the world of Phoebe's rugs who allowed her to have them photographed before her London exhibition in 1997, and without which there would have been no material for this book.

Many thanks must also go to Kaffe Fassett for his generous appreciation of Phoebe's work.

No book can be put together without the expertise and co-operation of a professional cast – in this case the design and production team at Cultureshock Media, led with heart-warming enthusiasm by the incomparable Fonz – Alfonso Iacurci – with the help of Hannah Dossary and Nicola Vanstone. Thank you all.